FEB -- '03

North Pole South Pole

Nancy Smiler Levinson

illustrated by
Diane Dawson Hearn

Weddell seal and young

Holiday House / New York

On the cover:
(top) polar bear;
(bottom) Emperor penguins

Text copyright © 2002 by Nancy Smiler Levinson
Illustrations copyright © 2002 by Diane Dawson Hearn
All Rights Reserved
Printed in the United States of America
www.holidayhouse.com
First Edition
Reading Level: 2.6

Library of Congress Cataloging-in-Publication Data
Levinson, Nancy Smiler.
North Pole, South Pole / by Nancy Smiler Levinson ;
illustrated by Diane Dawson Hearn.
p. cm.
Summary: An introduction to the geography, climate, and inhabitants
of the polar regions at the top and bottom of the earth where the
North Pole and the South Pole are located.
ISBN 0-8234-1737-9 (hardcover)
1. North Pole—Juvenile literature. 2. South Pole—Juvenile literature.
[1. North Pole. 2. South Pole.] I. Hearn, Diane Dawson ill. II. Title.
QH84.1 .L48 2002
508.311—dc21
2001059419

thick-billed murres

In summer the temperatures rise to
40 degrees *above* zero.
That is warm enough
to thaw a frozen fish.

harp seal

The earth tilts as it revolves
around the sun.
In winter the North Pole
tilts *away* from the sun.
The Arctic gets no daylight then.
From October to March
it is dark all the time.
In summer the North Pole
tilts *toward* the sun.
The sun never sets.
From April to September
it is light all the time.
You could go fishing
at midnight.

Arctic
summer

Arctic
winter

snowshoe hare

polar bear

arctic fox

Who is the king of animals
in the Arctic?
The mighty polar bear!
Whales, seals, and walrus
swim in the Arctic waters, too.

gray whale

walrus

harp seals

Land surrounds the Arctic Ocean.
The deep soil of the land
stays frozen all year.
No trees grow.
But mosses, flowers, and berries
grow every summer.

arctic wolf

arctic poppies

king eider duck

Caribou, arctic foxes, and wolves
make their home on Arctic land.
Ducks and seabirds come in summer.
They feed on fish, plants, and insects
near ocean shores.

white-rumped
sandpiper

caribou

rock ptarmigan

arctic
daisies

People have lived in the Far North
for thousands of years.
They hunt and fish for their food.
They made their clothing
and tents from animal skins.

Scientists and explorers come
to the North Pole, too.
They need layers of warm clothing.
They also need loads of food.
They eat chocolate
and peanut butter for energy.

The air is so dry,
they get very thirsty.
They need to melt enough ice
to drink three quarts of water a day.

black-browed albatross

SOUTH POLE

The South Pole is on land
surrounded by water.
This land is the continent
of Antarctica.
Most of it is covered with ice
that is two miles thick.
Even mountains, volcanoes, and lakes
are covered with ice.
Ice at the South Pole never melts.

chinstrap penguins

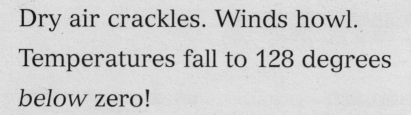

Dry air crackles. Winds howl.
Temperatures fall to 128 degrees
below zero!
Water freezes instantly.
Toothpaste and flashlight batteries
freeze.

Adélie penguins

Metal tools snap in half.

It is so cold that food never rots.

Antarctica is the coldest

place of all.

Antarctic seasons are the opposite
of seasons in the north.
June and July are the middle of winter.
It is dark all the time.
December and January
are the middle of summer.
There is daylight all the time.
Summer temperatures
at the South Pole
stay *below* zero.

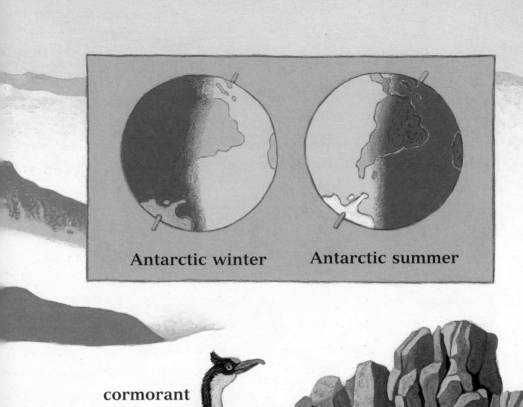

Antarctic winter   Antarctic summer

cormorant

No land animals live at the South Pole.
Only the Weddell seal and an insect
called the midge live in Antarctica
all year.
Penguins and other seabirds
come there in the summer months.
Penguins ride on moving ice floes.
Layers of fat keep them warm.
Tightly packed feathers keep them dry.

Weddell seals

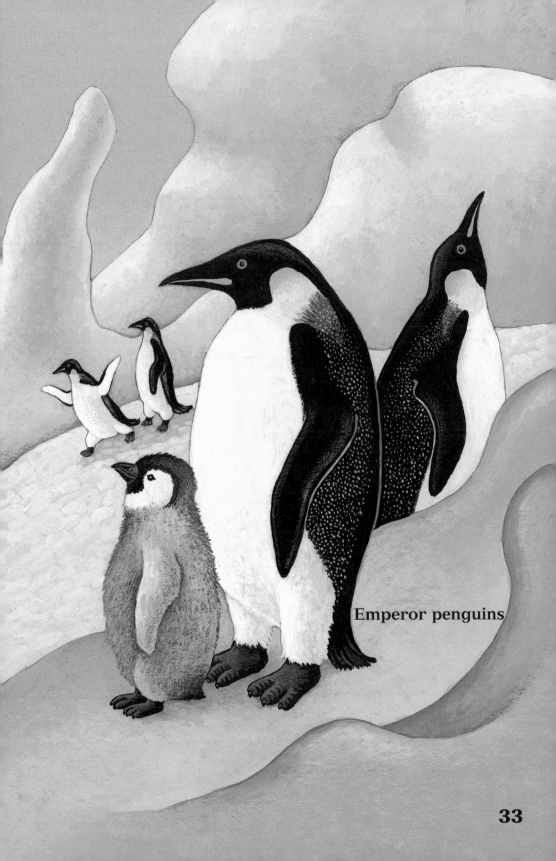

Emperor penguins

No people are native to Antarctica.
They could not have survived.
Now scientists from all over the world
come and live in research stations.
They need generators
to create power and heat.

They need all their food
delivered by air or sea.
They also need snowmobiles
to get from place to place.
On most winter days
they cannot go outside at all.

The North and South Poles
are places for scientists
to study the earth.
Scientists study the ice.
They study how weather changes
and how wildlife survives.
They study the earth's past
and think about its future.

They are looking for ways
to protect our earth
for all living things.

NORTH POLE

—It is in the Arctic.

—It is water surrounded by land.

—The average temperature
   in winter is 22 to 32 degrees below zero.

—The average temperature inland in summer
   is 32 to 50 degrees above zero.

—Winter months are October to March.

—Summer months are April to September.

—The first recorded explorer to reach the
   North Pole by dogsled was Admiral Robert
   E. Peary in 1909.

—The first pilot to fly over the North Pole
   was Admiral Richard E. Byrd in 1926.

SOUTH POLE

—It is in the Antarctic.

—It is on land surrounded by water.

—Antarctica is a continent.

—The average temperature of the interior in winter is 76 degrees below zero.

—The average temperature of the interior in summer is 14 degrees below zero.

—Winter months are April to September.

—Summer months are October to March.

—The first explorer to reach the South Pole by dogsled was Roald Amundsen in 1911.

—The first pilot to fly over the South Pole was Admiral Richard E. Byrd in 1929.

Acknowledgments

For their expert assistance and goodwill

in the preparation of this book, the author thanks

Linda Duguay, Director of Environmental Studies,

University of Southern California;

David Friscic, Technical Information Specialist,

Office of Polar Programs, National Science Foundation;

and Donal T. Manahan, Dean of Research,

College of Letters, Arts, and Sciences,

University of Southern California, and Chair,

Polar Research Board of National Academies.

baby harp seal